Fundamentals and Techniques of Pyrography

Basics of Materials, Tools, Techniques and Step by Step Instructions Project

Copyright © 2021

All rights reserved.

DEDICATION

The author and publisher have provided this e-book to you for your personal use only. You may not make this e-book publicly available in any way. Copyright infringement is against the law. If you believe the copy of this e-book you are reading infringes on the author's copyright, please notify the publisher at: https://us.macmillan.com/piracy

Contents

Pyrography 1

Basics of Supplies 4

List of Easy Wood Burning Ideas for Beginners 11

Techniques and Tricks 15

Simple Shading Pattern 28

Pyrography, Working in Layers 32

Carousel Horse Wood Burning 36

Pyrography Steps for Portrait Burning 40

Pyrography Feather Border 47

Pyrography

Pyrography or pyrogravure is the free handed art of decorating wood or other materials with burn marks resulting from the controlled application of a heated object such as a poker. It is also known as pokerwork or wood burning. [1]

The term means "writing with fire", from the Greek pur (fire) and graphos (writing).[2] It can be practiced using specialized modern pyrography tools, or using a metal implement heated in a fire, or even sunlight concentrated with a magnifying lens. "Pyrography dates from the 17th century and reached its highest standard in the 19th century. In its crude form it is pokerwork."[3]

A large range of tones and shades can be achieved. Varying the type of tip used, the temperature, or the way the iron is applied to the material all create different effects. After the design is burned in, wooden objects are often coloured. Light-coloured hardwoods such as sycamore, basswood, beech and birch are most commonly used, as their fine grain is not obtrusive. However, other woods, such as maple, pine or oak, are also used. Pyrography is also applied to leather items, using the same hot-iron technique. Leather lends itself to bold designs, and also allows very subtle shading to be achieved. Specialist vegetable-tanned leather must be used for pyrography (as modern tanning methods leave chemicals in the leather which are toxic when burned), typically in light colours for good contrast.

Pyrography is also popular among gourd crafters and artists, where designs are burned onto the exterior of a dried hard-shell gourd.

History

The process has been practiced by a number of cultures including the Egyptians and some African tribes since the dawn of recorded history[citation needed]. Pyrographer Robert Boyer hypothesizes that the art form dates back to prehistory when early humans created designs using the charred remains of their fires.[4] It was known in China from the time of the Han dynasty, where it was known as "Fire Needle Embroidery".[5] During the Victorian era, the invention of pyrography machines sparked a widespread interest in the craft, and it

Pyrography

was at this time that the term "pyrography" was coined (previously the name "pokerwork" had been most widely used)[6] In the late 19th century, a Melbourne architect by the name of Alfred Smart discovered that water-based paint could be applied hot to wood by pumping benzoline fumes through a heated hollow platinum pencil.[7] This improved the pokerwork process by allowing the addition of tinting and shading that were previously impossible. In the early 20th century, the development of the electric pyrographic hot wire wood etching machine further automated the pokerwork process, and Art Nouveau pyrographic gloveboxes and other works were popular in that era. Pyrography is a traditional folk art in many parts of Europe, including Romania, Poland, Hungary, and Flanders, as well as Argentina and other areas in South America.

Basics of Supplies

Woodburning pen. Quick note about the pen: I started out with this one: Walnut Hollow Value Pen. The heat is simply on/off, and it comes with 4 tips. After I lost a couple of the tips, I upgraded to this model: Walnut Hollow Versa Tool. It has variable heat control, which I like, as well as a case for the various tips. It's double the price, but still only $20! This is about as cheap and low-end as it gets, but has worked just fine for me for 6+ months. If you get really into pyrography, you can get pens that go into the hundreds of dollars.

Carbon paper

Tape

Sandpaper

Wet paper towel

Design or artwork to woodburn

Get Familiar With the Tool

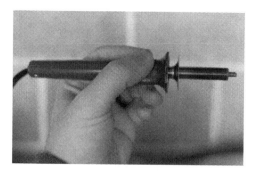

Pyrography

A woodburning pen is a very simple tool. It's a pen-like device with a metal end through which heat is transferred to a removable tip. All but the cheapest models are variable temperature tools. With any kit, you'll get 4-7 different tips for various methods of burning: straight lines, rounded lines, shading, etc. You'll also get a metal safety stand for the pen so it's never just sitting on a table or workbench.

The first thing you need to do, before working on any project, is to simply get familiar with the tool. Get a piece of scrap wood, plug in the woodburning tool and let it heat up for about 5 minutes, and test out "drawing" on the wood with the various tips just like you would with a pencil. It's that simple. (Be sure to let the tool cool down for 5 minutes before changing out tips; it'll then have to be heated up again for a few minutes.) The key is to go slow and steady. If you're jerky, it'll show. If you go too fast, the wood won't really burn like you want it to. Just like the tortoise, slow and steady wins the race.

Get familiar with the various tips. The one on the left is the rounded tip . it's probably the one I use the most. On the right is the shading tip; you'll notice it's flat bottom, so that you can burn a larger surface area at one time.

Pyrography

Get familiar with the various tips. The one on the left is the rounded tip — it's the one I use the most, and is pretty all-purpose. On the right is the shading tip; you'll notice its flat bottom, so that you can burn a larger surface area at one time.

A few other pointers to keep in mind:

I like to keep a wet paper towel on hand to wipe off the end of the tip every once in a while as residue from the wood builds up.

If you're getting a lot of smoke, the pen is too hot. Try turning down the heat for a smoother, smokeless burn.

Be mindful of safety. The tip gets extremely hot — several hundred degrees F, at minimum, in fact. So when the tool is plugged in, always be mindful of where the hot metal end is. Be sure it isn't touching anything and always have it resting on the metal stand when not in use. When changing tips, use pliers wrapped in electrical tape, as the tips stay hot for a long time.

Pyrography

Choose a Design

For my first project, I chose the above design of a quaint cabin in the mountains. The options are limitless for what you can burn onto a piece of a wood. So far, I've worked with basic, black and white designs, but as I get better, I'm sure I'll get into more advanced shading techniques and whatnot.

To find designs and patterns to work with, just google anything you're interested in with "black and white illustration" added to the end: "mountains black and white illustration," "wildlife black and white illustration," "Minnesota Vikings black and white illustration." You'll more than likely get some great results to choose from.

After you've picked a design, you want to figure out the size you want to use as well. For this above design, I sized it to fit a piece of wood I

Pyrography

already had. The other few I've done I just made the size of an 8.5×11" sheet of paper, since that's what I can easily print here at home.

Find and Prep the Wood

You can really use any wood for your pyrography project. Soft woods will burn at lower temps, while harder woods will take a very hot pen. The piece in the picture is pine — very easy to work with. To prep your wood, if it's a "raw" piece like this, you'll want to sand it very well, and also decide which way you want the grain. It's much easier to burn with the grain than against it. With my cabin project, it had more horizontal lines than vertical, so I kept the grain horizontal.

You can also use pre-fab wood projects like boxes or pre-cut shapes

Pyrography

that you can find at any hobby store. You'll see later in the article how I used those. Anything pre-fab you buy at a hobby store will be very easy to work with, and you won't have to worry about grain as much.

Affix Your Design to the Wood

Cabin in the mountains woodburning.

Tape your cut out design (a broad outline is fine as long as it fits on the wood) to the carbon paper, and then to the wood.

Trace Your Design

Using a pen, firmly trace the outline of your design.

Pyrography

Woodburning tracing outline.

After tracing, it should look something like this.

Burn the Outline

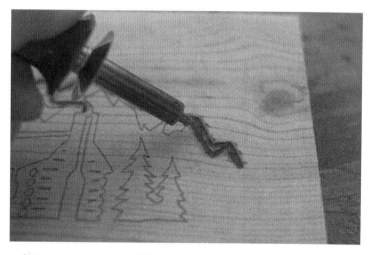

Get started! Using the pen, follow the carbon line you just traced onto the wood. Again, go with the grain as much as you can. This was my first project, so you can sort of see some lines in the burn where I was a little jerky.

List of Easy Wood Burning Ideas for Beginners

1) Woodburning Cutting Board

Cutting boards make great gifts and are necessary to have in any kitchen. To start making a wood burned cutting board, trace your design onto the surface in whatever configuration suits your design.

The artist in the video uses a dog pattern and places it in the right corner of the cutting board, but you can use any design you like and choose to center or off center it as you see fit.

Pyrography

Once the pattern is transferred onto your burning surface, use a linework pen tip to burn the basic outline of the pattern. Fill in the design with a shader tip and add details based on the natural shadows and contours of your pattern.

2) Dragonfly Board

For this project you will need a small board and a dragonfly pattern. A similar pattern can be found online on etsy.com or other art suppliers. You can also freehand draw your design. The artist in the video combines two stencils, so there is no right or wrong way to get your project started. Once the pattern is on the wood, burn all the linework with a line tip.

Pyrography

Use a shader tip to apply shading where you would like. For a colorful finished project, fill in your design using colored pencils and seal in the color with a clear finishing product.

3) Floral Eggs

This project requires wooden eggs, which can be found at art supply stores or online. The artist recommends working the floral pattern free hand to make unique designs and shapes. She begins by burning a small circle with a line tip, and then makes petals around the circle.

She continues to add overlapping flowers on the egg and rotates the egg and the pyrography pen as she works to make linework easier. This project is great for practicing linework and can be sold in art shows.

Throughout the process, the artist keeps her pen heat high to make the project easier and faster. If you would like to add color to your wood burning, you can fill in the flowers with watercolor paint. Finish with a clear gloss to add shine and protect the paint.

Pyrography

4) Basic Moose

Start this project with a light-colored, square board. The artist uses bamboo, but any light wood will work. Free hand draw or use a stencil to apply a moose outline onto the board. Use a knife tip or other flat edge tip to create the lines of the moose.

Once your outline is burned, use a basic lighter to fill in the moose body. You can also use your pyrography pen and a shader tip, but a lighter will get the job done faster.

5) Woodburning Spoons

Wood burned spoons make a great gift for the cook in your life, and can be easily sold at art shows. In this tutorial, the artist transfers word stencils into the bowls of the spoons.

Once the main lettering work is complete, the artist free hand burns small shapes and designs into the necks and handles of the spoons

Pyrography

Techniques and Tricks

1 – INVEST IN THE RIGHT TOOLS.

A good wood burning tool is one that is lightweight and easy to hold. This tool is ideal for wood burning letters and designs, as it is easy to hold and manipulate. It comes with several nice tips to use in projects: a chisel tip (my personal favorite), a cone-shaped tip, a rounded tip, and a teardrop-shaped tip. Wood burning for beginners is so much easier with the proper tool on hand!

In addition to the tool above, strongly recommend purchasing a set of letter tips for wood burning letters on personalized projects. These tips make adding monograms, names and inscriptions to projects so much easier than doing it freehand. used a set of letter tips with my wood burning tool for my monogrammed wood keychains.

2 – IF POSSIBLE, AVOID WOOD BURNING PROJECTS AROUND KIDS AND PETS.

To say that wood burning tools get hot is a serious understatement. Severe burns can happen in an instant, and working with these tools requires a great level of caution and diligence. One of my best wood burning tips: only work on pyrography projects when children and pets are not going to have immediate access to your wood burning tools!

3 – NEVER LEAVE A WOOD BURNING TOOL UNATTENDED.

Related to #2 above, pyrography tools are incredibly hot, and they should not be left unattended, even for a few minutes.

4 – ALWAYS USE THE STAND WHEN SETTING THE WOOD BURNING TOOL DOWN WHILE IN USE.

One thing love about the tool linked above in tip #1 is that it comes equipped with a handy stand for propping up the tool while in use. Never lay the heat burning pen on a table or other surface, as it will burn the surface in an instant!

Pyrography

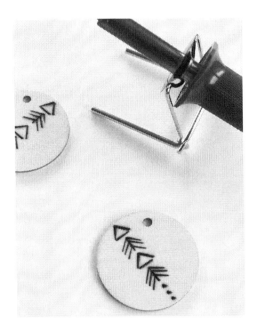

5 – NEVER TOUCH THE TIP OF THE WOOD BURNING TOOL, EVEN JUST AFTER INSTALLING A NEW TIP.

Word to the wise: the tips on these tools heat up nearly instantaneously, so NEVER touch a heat tool tip with your bare hands, even one that has just been inserted.

6 – TO REMOVE/ADD A TIP, HOLD TIP WITH PLIERS AND TWIST THE TOOL TO LOOSEN/TIGHTEN.

A nice pair of flat-nosed jewelry pliers is the very best tool to use for adding and removing tips from a heat burning tool. Never attempt to do so with your bare hands! To add or remove a tip, hold the tip firmly in the pliers, and twist the tool itself–and not the tip–to loosen/tighten.

7 – HAVE A BOWL OF COLD WATER READY FOR INSTANTLY COOLING USED TIPS.

Instantly cool hot tips in a bowl of cold water to prevent burns on hands and work surfaces. Be sure to wipe tips dry before reinserting into the tool.

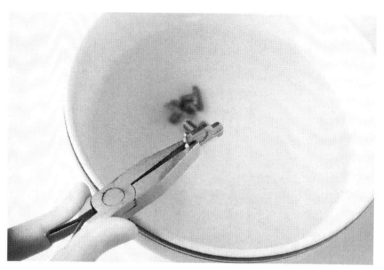

8 – PRESS LIGHTLY.

Avoid the urge to press too hard when working with a tool for wood burning letters and designs. Often, it takes just a second for the wood burning tool to do its job!

9 – PRACTICE, PRACTICE, PRACTICE!

One of my best pyrography tips: always practice with the tool on a surface of the same material as your finished project before starting on the final project. Different woods respond to the heat tool in different ways, so learning how much pressure to apply, how long to hold the tool against the surface of the wood, etc., is critical to the success of a finished project. I often will use the same tip to create a number of the same design over and over again until I instinctively know just the right amount of pressure and how much time is required to get the desired result.

When using the wood burning pen, hold it as you would a regular pen in your dominant hand. Press the surface of the tip evenly against the surface of the wood, holding just until the heat of the tip penetrates the wood. There might be a little bit of smoke, and that is okay! Just make sure not to hold the tip against the wood too long, as it is possible to burn through the wood entirely.

The chisel tip is my absolute favorite, as it creates straight lines quickly and easily simply by holding the tip flat against a surface, as I did to create the honeycomb design below in my wood burned earrings. You can also use the sharp point of the chisel for more intricate, detailed

Pyrography

wood burned designs.

10 – USE STENCIL DESIGNS AS A TEMPLATE.

Freehanded designs and letter and number tips are not the only options for creating show-stopping wood burning projects. Another fun idea is to trace a stencil design onto the wood surface with a pencil, and then use the wood tool to outline and fill in the design. (Avoid tracing around a plastic or paper stencil directly with the wood burning tool, as the tool will melt or burn the stencil.)

With these pyrography tips, your wood burning projects are sure to be a success! For even more wood burning insight, check out this helpful post from The Art of Manliness.

WOOD BURNING TIPS AND TOOLS

1. Consider purchasing a wood burning tip/pen combination woodburner.

If you plan to switch tips frequently, a tip/pen combination woodburner can save you time. Pyrography burners can reach temperatures of 750 to 1050 degrees Fahrenheit (400 to 565 Celsius). Burners that use the screw-style, solid point tips, typically use soft brass metal. This metal can take five minutes or more to cool down to a temperature where you can remove the tip safely with just your fingers. While you can reduce this time by using pliers, this is not recommended since you can easily strip the threads on this soft metal if you try to remove the tip when it is still hot.

However, on wire-nib burners that use a tip/pen combination, you can replace the entire handle even when the tips are hot. You do not need to wait until the tip cools. This can be a big convenience if you need to use different tips on one project.

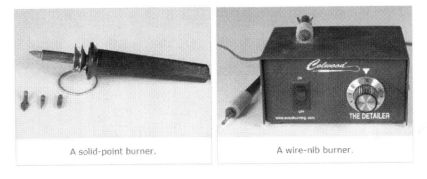

A solid-point burner.   A wire-nib burner.

2. Realize that smaller gauge tips typically take longer to heat up. When it comes to wire gauges, the general rule is the smaller the gauge number, the thicker the wire. With pyrography tools, you should notice it takes longer to heat a thicker wire. For example, a 16-gauge tip would take longer to heat up than a 20-gauge tip.

Pyrography

3. Be able to identify the following "wire-nib" woodburning tips and best uses for these tips.

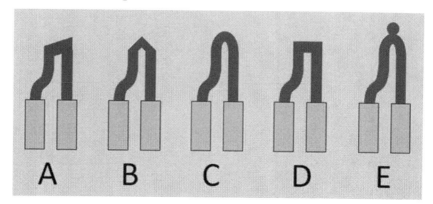

Skew tip (A) has an angled or slanted burning tip. Many people frequently use this tip for long running lines, like burning large feathers. Spear tip (B) – has a pointed edge. Many people use this tip for getting into tight places and for burning fine details. Round tip (C) – has a circular point. This tip is desirable when a depression is not wanted. Chisel tip (D) has a burning edge that is perpendicular to the side edges. Many people use this tip for running quill lines. Ballpoint tip (E) – has a tiny ball welded to the tip end. Many people use this tip when a natural writing motion is wanted.

4. Be able to identify the following "solid-point" woodburning tips and best uses for these tips.

Pyrography

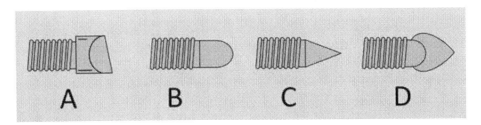

Many people use the all-purpose (universal) tip (A) for burning the outline of designs and for creating straight lines. The calligraphy tip (B) is good for curved lines and for natural writing. The extra fine tip (C) is typically used for detailed work, straight lines, and creating tighter curves. Many people use the shading tip (D) for filling and shading large areas and adding shadows.

5. Realize that softer, lower density, woods such as basswood tend to burn faster
and require less heat than harder, denser woods. See Appendix A and B for a list of woods and their densities. Basswood is also a popular wood for burning because it has very little grain, and the burning creates a sharp contrast between the original wood and the deep color of the burning. On the other hand, hard woods like ash, maple, and oak tend to require more heat and burn slower.

6. Avoid stroke marks when shading an area with a gradient fill

Pyrography

— by working on medium heat using circular movements. This will slowly darken in an area. Burning a gradient fill is more difficult than simply filling in black. It takes less heat and more patience.

7. Consider following the sequence that most woodburners use.
Most woodburners first prepare the piece by sanding the wood to a smooth finish. Next they transfer or draw a design on the wood — possibly using graphite paper, carbon paper, or a soft pencil. Next, they burn the outlines, and finally adding filling and shading.

8. First burn the outline of the design when staining.
By burning the outlines, the wood is "somewhat" sealed off from the rest of the wood. Now you can apply stain without worrying about stain bleeding into the surrounding areas.

9. Burn with the grain when possible for an easier operation.
Most woodburners find it easier to go with the grain than trying to work against it. Burning against the grain typically offers up more resistance.

10. Avoid pressing down too hard on the workpiece with the

Pyrography

woodburning tip.

Contrary to what many beginners feel, a lot of pressure is not necessary to successfully burn wood. In fact, light pressure allows you to guide the pen carefully to create graceful strokes. The light pressure also results in fewer errors and less accidental burns. Let the woodburning tips do the work, rather than forcing them. Furthermore, keep in mind, too much pressure can bend hot tips.

11. Avoid fumes when burning wood.

Burning wood can create fumes that can cause serious health problems. To help avoid inhaling fumes, work outside or in well-ventilated area. If working in a non-ventilated area, a smoke capturing/extracting device is recommended similar to the GourdMaster Woodburning Buddy II.

12. Use a round wood burning tip when burning if you want to change directions easily.

Round tips or ball tips do not sink as deeply into the wood as other types of tips. This gives you more freedom of movement and allows you to change directions easily. These features make these tips excellent for writing and signing. On the other hand, chisel tips, skew

Pyrography

tips, and spear tips are more difficult to change directions.

13. Avoid pressure-treated wood, Medium Density Fiber (MDF), and wood which has been stained or finished when burning.

Pressure-treated wood contains chemical preservatives which help protect the wood from termites, fungal decay, and insects. Similarly, Medium Density Fiber (MDF) boards contain unsafe chemicals and formaldehyde. Finally, stains and finishes are also likely to contain chemicals that when burned can emit harmful fumes. However, most experts consider the outer layer of plywood safe for woodburning. Plywood is composed of three or more thin layers of wood bonded together using an adhesive. If burning only the outer layers of plywood (avoiding the adhesive), then it is safe material for woodburning.

14. Realize that most 110-volt electric branding irons will take 15-20 minutes to reach operating temperature.

An electric branding iron.

The impression created using this branding iron.

Once this temperature has been reached, the branding iron should be

Pyrography

able to make a good, dark impression in wood in about 2-4 seconds. Non-electric branding irons (typically heated with a propane torch) can reach operating temperatures in 2-3 minutes. However, unlike electric branding irons, non-electric branding irons require reheating between impressions.

15. Realize that for a branding iron to work, the area has to be dead flat.

When creating an impression on the bottom of a bowl, a smaller design typically works better. This is because instead of creating a "perfectly flat" bottom, many woodturners create a shallow undercut from the rim of the base to the center of the base. This undercut ensures that the piece will sit only on the rim and will stand without wobbling even if the wood slightly moves over time. If given the choices shown below, a woodturner would more likely find a flat spot on the bottom of the piece using the smaller branding iron "Design #2". This smaller design could also be "rocked" back and forth easier on the wood to help create the impression.

Simple Shading Pattern

Long, pulled shading stroke

Using a wide, flat burning tip as the spear shader or curved edge shader, set the edge of your shader on the practice board and with slow, even motion pull the shader through the area to be burned. The pen tip will naturally begin the line burn with a dark tonal value. As you pull the tip edge across the board the tip will lose heat and the tonal value of the stroke will fade. This creates a simple line that starts dark and gradually goes to a very pale tone.

The time you allow the pen tip to lie on the wood at the beginning of this stroke determines how dark the tonal value will be. In the sample squares below the first, left hand, square was worked with a quick, flowing start to the stroke. The second, center, square the edge of the shader was set then pulled across the board.

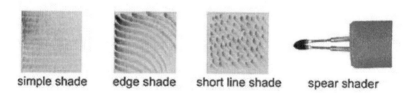

simple shade   edge shade   short line shade   spear shader

Practice board daisy pattern

Pyrography

This practice board sample, using a daisy pattern, was worked in three layers of burning. All of the shading in the daisy petal, leaves, and stems was worked using the spear shader and the long, pulled shading stroke.

Step 1 – Sand your board, trace your pattern
Lightly sand your practice board with 220- to 320- grit sandpaper, remove any sanding dust with a dry, clean cloth. Trace your pattern to the wood.

Step 2 – Map your tonal value shading areas
Set your wood burning unit to a medium-low or low-medium temperature setting. Using the spear shader and following the photo below, work a layer of long, pull strokes into the design. In the petals start your stroke where the petal is closest to the flower center or where it tucks under another petal. The shading for the leaves begins at the central vein of the leave and is pulled towards the outer edge. In the darkest toned leave areas a second set of long, pulling strokes are worked from the leaf edge towards the first central vein lines.

Pyrography

Step 3 – Deepen your tonal values with a new layer of strokes

Working one layer of burning over another deepens the tonal values of an area. You can slowly, and carefully develop the exact shades of sepia you want by working in layers. In the photo, below, a second layer of long, pill strokes has been worked. The temperature setting has been raised slightly to a medium to mid-medium setting. Even on such a low temperature setting, the second layer has created very dark tonal values in several areas of the pattern.

The flower center is surrounded with a ring of small flowers or fuzz. A touch-and-lift dot pattern has been worked to imply the center spots of those small flowers. You can use your spear shader tip to create this dot pattern, it will burn very small black triangles.

long pull shading 3

Step 4 – Add low temperature accent and detailing lines

Pyrography

For this simple daisy pattern two layers of shading was enough to create pale, medium, and dark tonal shades inside the petals and leaves. To separate the unburned white areas of the petal tips from the unburned background wood ,set your temperature setting to a low heat. Using either the ball tip or looped tip pen create thin, pale lines along these areas.

Do not completely outline all of your pattern lines. When the petal or leave starts to show a burned tonal value along the outer edge stop your accent line. The shading is enough to define that area of the pattern.

Add the inside detail lines – the fold lines in the petals, the vein lines in your leaves.

Pyrography, Working in Layers

Developing your burning with layers

There are many ways to approach a wood burning project. You might chose to separate your design into several distinct tonal values as the Bengal Tiger project is worked or you may wish to map the design working from the darkest tonal values to the bright highlights just as the Flamingo portrait has been burned. As the Sea Dragon is worked you may wish to focus of the basic shapes of each area to create your finished project.

No matter which approach you chose the burning process is developed by laying one layer of burning over another to slowly bring each area up to its final tonal value. Working the entire design in low or medium temperature burnings then adding new layers of burning over the first gives you total control over your final tonal values.

Step 1: First, low temperature burn
Low temperature burning to establish darkest tonal areas

This little red hen has chosen an old apple basket for her egg nest. Because of the number of elements within this design this fun, folk art

Pyrography

style pattern is a great practice piece to learn layer work. The first layer of burning has been done on a low temperature setting, 5.5 for my wood burning unit, and with the standard writing tip. you have used a tight short line stroke in the basket and the hen feathers. The apples are worked using a tight random doodle stroke.

you have worked to establish the basic shading areas that will shape the hen's round body, the basket's curve and the round shape of the apples. The spokes of the basket lie behind the horizontal ribs, so they also need an early shading to place them towards the background of the pattern.

As this is a folk art styled design want lots of detail and texture so have begun working a little shading into each of the hen's feathers. As deepen the tones in this area later with more layers of burning this early detailing will also become darker.

Notice that there are no extremely dark or pale tones. This first layer falls in the pale mid-range of your sepia value scale. For me this early work gives me a chance to think through the design considering where my darkest tones will be needed to push elements back into the final burning and where my highlights will fall to bring areas forward.

Pyrography

Step 2: Second, medium temperature burn

you have established the general shape and positions of the elements with the first layer of burning. Now you begin to refine those shapes and position shadows with deeper tones towards the mid-tone range of the sepia scale. you have turned my burning unit up to a 6.

you have darkened the hen's body where she sits against her eggs, the straw and the apples. This darker tone pushes her body down into the basket. The bottom areas of the apples have been worked to a dark mid-tone value to push them behind the hen's body. The hen's eggs now have a few random doodle speckles added.

The spokes and ribs of the basket have had some wood grain texture

Pyrography

added. you have used a very tight short line stroke to create the grain lines. you have used that same stroke to create the sides of the holes in the wood spokes. The staples that bind the ribs are not burned. Instead you have worked the area around them by adding a shadow to the ribs and a small dark spot where the staple enters the wood.

Carousel Horse Wood Burning

Step 1:

You will need your wood burning tool, a 9" x 12" basswood blank, a glazed tile on which to rest the tool, sand paper, tracing paper, water color pencils, scotch tape, and polyurethane spray sealer.

Sand the project board well before beginning any of the burning steps. Wipe with a clean cloth to remove the dust.

Rub the back of the pattern paper with the lead from a soft pencil. Tape the pattern to the project board and trace over the design lines.

Once the pattern has been transferred to the wood you can go over the pattern lines with your pencil to darken them as needed.

Pyrography

Step 2:

Using the side of the wood burning tools begin with the shading on the horse's body. Note here that the two back legs are burned slightly darker than the foreground legs. The belly area also has extra darkness to it.

The center areas of each of the body parts have been left at the natural tones of the wood. This gives a feeling of roundness to the horse.

Step 3:

Using the blade edge of the wood burning tool outline the horse's body. Roll the tool between your thumb and forefinger to make the

Pyrography

lines curve.

Step 4:

Shading has been added to the horse's mane and tail as well as to his saddle, bridle, and accents. Use the tool on it's side. Change the coloring of the shading as you work. Some areas may have very dark shading where others might have a lighter tone. This adds interest to the work.

Step 5:

The detailing to the mane, tail, saddle, bridle and accents have been done. Study the close up photo of the horse for ideas on how each was accomplished.

Step 6:

Pyrography

Coloring is easily added by using colored pencils over wood burned designs. I have used water color pencils that are applied as any other colored pencil except that they can then be blended with a small amount of water on a soft brush. This blending step takes away any lines left from the pencil work.

Because the pencil has a solid firm point only the top surface of the burning is colored letting all of your wood burning details and shading remain.

Once the coloring is complete give the piece several light coats of a polyurethane spray sealer, following the manufacturer's instructions.

Pyrography Steps for Portrait Burning

Working with skin and hair

Supplies:

8 ½"x 12" x ¼" birch plywood

Variable temperature wood burning unit

Standard writing tip

Graphite paper

White artist eraser

#2 soft pencil

This Pixie Queen burning will allow you to practice creating the human face before you begin wood burning portraits from family and friend photos. Because our Pixie is a mythical creature you can learn to burn soft skin tones, shaping the facial features and creating crisp eyes

Pyrography

without worrying about being totally true to a particular person's facial features.

The focus of the project is contrast in tonal values that lie side by side. The pale tones of the face are framed by the black tones of the background trapped hair on the right side of her face. The ruffles of the almost white clothing capture black tone shadows. The deep toned pine cones rest on pale blonde hair. Throughout the burning I will be placing very dark tones in direct contact with extremely pale areas.

Begin your project by lightly sanding your board with 220-grit sand paper. Remove any sanding dust with a clean tack cloth. Trace the pattern to the board using graphite paper or by rubbing the back of the pattern paper with a soft #2 pencil. As you trace along the pattern lines the pencil rubbing will leave a fine gray line that can be erased after burning.

Step 1: Darkest points in the face

This entire project was worked on low-medium and medium

Pyrography

temperature settings using the standard writing tip. A tight flowing random doodle stroke was used for the face shading, long line strokes for the hair and cross hatching for the dress areas. Low temperatures with multiple layers of burning will bring the darkest areas up to their tonal values.

you want the skin tones as even and smooth as possible so throughout this project working at as low a temperature as you can so the color develops very slowly. The constant motion of the random doodle avoids the small hot spots that can happen with line strokes as cross hatching. This particular burning stroke can be worked with wide turn back loops that allow a large amount of un-burned area between the bends or, as will be using on this project, with tight turns that cover the entire working area. Within several layers of burning the shading will blend into gradual shading through the face.

have started the mapping of the face to find my shadow areas. The darkest points in her face are the corners of the mouth, the inner corners of the eyes, the nostrils, and inside of her ears. My light source is coming from the upper left hand corner so the left side of her face will be lighter in tonal value than the right with the darkest skin tones

Pyrography

along the right cheek and jaw line.

Step 2: Mapping the highlights

When you map an area you're looking for my darkest tonal values in the element that working. By burning these dark areas first at a low temperature can easily add and expand the shading to include the mid-tone and pale values that will need to create the dimension of the object. All of my shading is worked off this first mapping of the dark tones. At the same time want to make note of where my brightest, unburned highlights will fall in the object. Since these areas will not be worked on the project often will make pencil notes on my paper pattern for reference as work.

This photo comes several steps from now but it is a good example of

Pyrography

the finished shading on the face. As work the first shading steps on the skin also want to map where my highlights will fall. These highlight area are unburned so that they remain the tonal value of the raw wood.

The highest point in the face is the nose with the forehead, eye brow ridges, cheeks and chin falling below this point. The nose bridge, eye lids, corner of the nose and chin sit deeply into the face. The eyes are the deepest point.

For our Pixie there are three vertical lines that run from her jaw line to her hair line. The brightest highlights fall directly on these lines. Because her head is tilted to the right the first highlight lines begins high on the forehead and runs to the top of her cheek before the jaw line rolls away from the light source. Where this line hits the high areas of the face there will be a bright highlight.

The second vertical begins a little left of the center of her forehead and runs through her nose to the top of her chin. This line does not run directly down the center of her nose but towards the left of center because of her head tilt. The final vertical line starts low of the forehead and stops at the top edge of the corner of her mouth. The forehead area above this line rolls away from the light source and the area below the mouth to the bottom edge of the chin also drops away from the light.

With the light coming from the upper left to the face that highlights in the first, left, line will be larger than those in the center vertical line with the highlights in the right line being small and compact.

Step 3: Deepening the tonal values and shading the neck

you've added a second layer of shading to the face which has darkened the first mapped areas and added a medium tone shading along her jaw line, ears and eye lid areas. The neck area has been worked. Because her collar folds behind her neck a medium tonal value is needed to distinguish these two areas. The shading under the left side of the neck accents the highlight areas that will fall on the edge of the left jaw line and the left side of the chin.

Step 4: Adding the eye pupils, inner ear shadow and the corners of the mouth

The mouth has been detailed; notice how dark the corners of the mouth have become. The ear also has its detailing so that the inside ear will be as dark as the eye pupils. The nostrils are made with just a line because of the tilt of her head very little of the nostrils show.

The eyes are worked by first lightly shading the entire eye ball area. The eye is an actual ball shape that is set behind the eye brow ridge and the cheek bone area. The eye is the deepest area of the face so the eye needs to be shaded. Once the shading was done the iris and pupil were added. A hint of eyelashes and one fine line for the eyebrow complete the eyes. Very fine lines add a feeling of eye lashes along the upper eye lids.

Pyrography Feather Border

Supply List:

9" x 10" birch plywood board

220- or 320- grit sandpaper

graphite paper

pencil and ruler

variable temperature wood burning unit

ball tip pen

spear shader pen

curved shader pen

masking or painter's tape

brown paper bag

artist quality colored pencils

gloss or semi-gloss spray sealer

Prepare your wood blank

Lightly sand your wood project using 220- or 320- grit sandpaper to remove any loose wood fibers and imperfections. Sand with the grain of the wood to avoid creating fine swirl scratches that sandpaper can leave. Wipe the wood surface with a dry, clean cloth to remove any dust.

Pyrography

On a scrap piece of the same wood, leather, or gourd media that you will be burning create a sepia practice board scale that is divided into ten units. We will be using that scale throughout this project for the tonal values and temperature settings.

Trace the pattern

Click and save a copy of this free pyrography pattern by Lora Irish to your computer. Print a copy to use in this tracing step.

Measure the geometric line design on the pattern. Use a ruler and pencil to mark the geometric pattern to your board. This geometric board is a simple 3/8" thick line, a 1/8" unburned margin, and a 7/8" wide line of triangles. A seven triangle repeat measures at 6 3/8" on

Pyrography

the inside edge of the board.

Center the paper pattern to your board and secure one edge with masking or painter's tape. Slide a sheet of graphite tracing paper under the pattern and trace along the outlines using an ink pen. Check that you have all lines transferred and remove the pattern paper and graphite paper.

Wood Burning Step 1 – Shaping the feathers
Click on any of the project images for a large image that you can save to your computer.

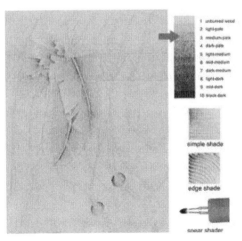

The first step for our feather border is to create the basic shape or curve of the feather. This step uses a spear shader, the long pull stroke, and a tonal value setting for medium-pale. Each side of the feathers is an upside-down cup. From the center feather shaft the feather side curves up to the center line of that part of the feather and then drops down to the outer edge.

Begin your spear shader strokes at the feather shaft and pull towards the central area of the feather in a long, curving line. The stroke will naturally be darkest where you begin your stroke and fade into a very pale tone as it nears the mid-portion of the feather side.

Use the spear shader and the long pull stroke to work long lines into the fur clusters at the top of the feathers. This shading is worked where one cluster of fur tucks under another and is pulled from the tucked point of the cluster towards the outer edge of that cluster. Again, allow your stroke lines to curve.

The beads are shaded along the sides, working towards the center of the bead using the long pull stroke and spear shader.

Wood Burning Step 2 – Shading the edge of the wood burned feathers

Pyrography

To curve and shape the outer edges of the feathers use the spear shader on a slightly hotter temperature setting for a pale-medium tonal value. Place the side of the spear shader against the outer edge pattern line and burn long pull strokes that curve towards the center area of the feather side. Match the curve of this series of strokes to the curve of the strokes made in the previous step. Each feather side should now go from dark along the outer edge, gradually fading to a pale or unburned wood tone at the center of the feather side, and then gradually darken as it nears the feather shaft.

Wood Burning Step 3 – Shading the leather strings

Using the spear shader and the long pull stroke, shade the leather strings at the top where they wrap around the two feather shafts, and below the feathers in the beaded area of the leather. The shading is worked from where the leather tucks under either the feather or into the bead, then pulled towards the center point of that section of string. Use a pale-medium to mid-medium temperature setting for this step.

Shade the feather shafts using the long pull stroke. The darkest shadow on the shafts falls on the left side of the feather.

Pyrography

Wood Burning Step 4 – Creating a drop shadow
Creating a drop shadow in your pyrography projects

A drop shadow is worked in the background area of the design and pushes your elements visually off the wood. This step creates those drop shadows on the left side of the feathers and leather strings. They are created with the ball tip or looped tip pen, a pale-medium tonal value, and either a solid-fill stroke texture or a tightly packed scrubbie stroke.

Drop shadows are never darker than the tonal value of the area that is creating them. As we develop the feather in the next few steps you will see that the outer edge of the feather will have a tonal value about two steps deeper than the shadow we are now creating. Please refer to the finished pyrography project at the top of this post.

The wider the drop shadow, the farther from the background your element hangs. Narrow shadows place your element close to the background. Note in the image the point on the far left feather shadow and the point on the actual feather. The space between these two points defines the distance that the actual feather is from the

Pyrography

background wood. This space is a visual measurement or reference.

The amount of air space between the shadow and the element defines the distance of the element from the board. The leather strings hang free – do not touch – the background. We know that because the shadow does not touch the leather string. The beads do touch, lie against, the background. We know this because the shadow touches the bead and is only a partial circle, not a full shaped shadow. In the feathers, returning to the left feather point, we know that this feather does not touch the background because the two points – feather and shadow – are so far apart.

Made in the USA
Columbia, SC
06 December 2022